The Official MotoGP™ Annual 2016

Written by Hazel Jackson
Designed by Chris Dalrymple

A Grange Publication

ISBN 978-1-910199-67-1

Contents

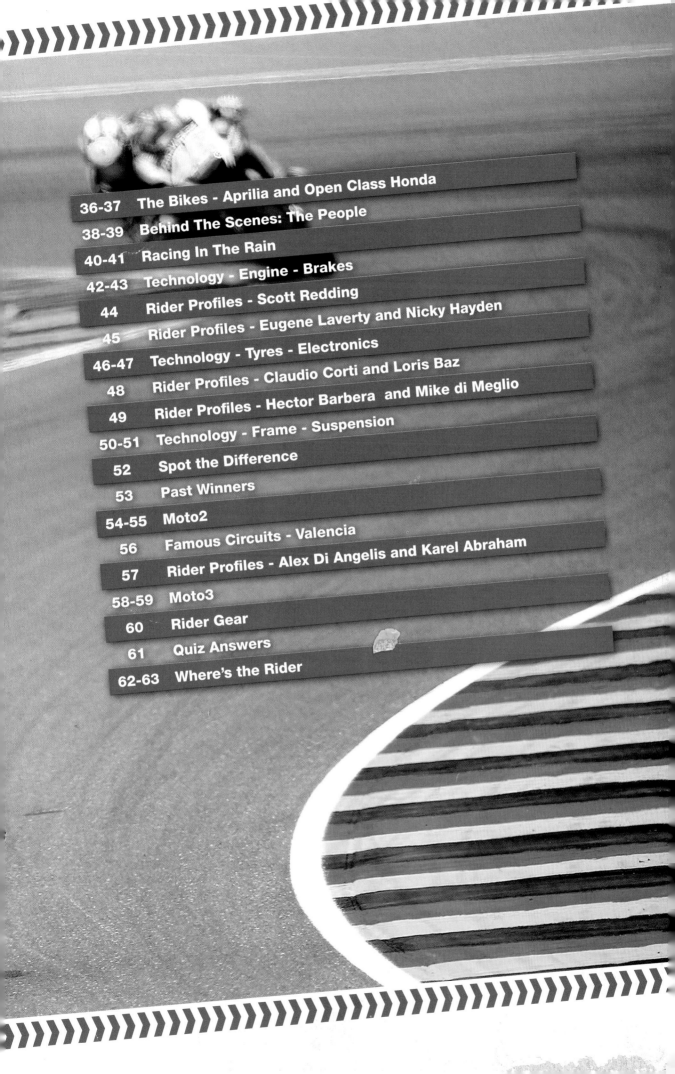

))))) The World's fastest riders
))))) The World's fastest bikes

Welcome to MotoGP – the world championship Grand Prix for motorcycle racing, the most exciting sport ever. The world's fastest riders race against each other on the fastest motorcycles in the world. There are 18 spectacular race meetings held in 13 different countries and riders try and score as many points as they can at every race and, at the end of the year, the one with most points wins the title of World Champion.

How do men win the title? By having a fast motorcycle and a really strong team of mechanics to work on the bike all year round and prepare it painstakingly for every single race. They also need to have the willpower to outthink and outclass their rivals on the track and they must be physically fit and strong. The fastest motorcycles in the world take huge strength to handle, but the guy who wins the mantle of World Champion has to have that special something extra, and that's the self belief that they can defeat everybody else.

The FIM MotoGP World championship started in 1949 and men have fought for the title ever since. The motorcycles have changed a lot in the last 67 years, becoming more powerful and using new technology to make them safer to ride. However, the bikes have always been 'prototypes' which means they are built especially for the championship.

Point Scoring

At every race only the top 15 finishers score points and there are 140 points awarded at each meeting. This is how they are divided up:

1st Place	25 pts
2nd Place	20 pts
3rd Place	16 pts
4th Place	13 pts
5th Place	11 pts
6th Place	10 pts
7th Place	9 pts
8th Place	8 pts
9th Place	7 pts
10th Place	6 pts
11th Place	5 pts
12th Place	4 pts
13th Place	3 pts
14th Place	2 pts
15th Place	1 pts

You won't see MotoGP bikes anywhere but at MotoGP races and you can't buy them in shops. They're not built to be ridden on the road like normal motorcycles and you'll notice that they don't have headlights, indicators or number plates! Instead they are built to be very, very fast. That doesn't just mean powerful engines. Race circuits have tight, twisting corners and long sweeping bends and these mean the bike must have good brakes, so that it can stop quickly, safely and be easy to steer into and out of corners. In MotoGP, being able to approach a corner quicker than another rider and brake later than them lets the rider overtake his competitors, so this is very important. All the companies that make MotoGP motorcycles work; Honda, Yamaha, Suzuki, Ducati and Aprilia, employ the cleverest men they can find to work very hard all year round to try and make their motorcycles better and faster than the competition.

The bikes also showcase the design and technological capabilities of their manufacturers. The machines are therefore constructed from expensive, hardwearing and extremely light materials such as titanium and reinforced carbon fibre and benefit from the sort of advanced technology (carbon disk brakes, engine management systems, traction control), which doesn't feature on regular road bikes.

»»»»»» Valentino Rossi »

Team: Movistar Yamaha
Nationality: Italian
Age: 36

Valentino Rossi is the most famous motorcycle racer in the world and has won an amazing 9 world championship titles. He won the 125cc GP class (which became Moto3) in 1997 and the 250GP class (now Moto2) in 1999. He moved to the MotoGP class in 2000 riding a Honda, and won the championship the very next year – and kept on winning. He left Honda to ride for Yamaha and won his very first race on the new bike! He then went to ride for Ducati for two years – but things didn't go well on that bike, so he decided to come back to Yamaha and started winning races again. Valentino is also very popular with race fans all over the world and earns a lot of money – over $34 million per year – by helping companies promote their products – for example by drinking their drinks on the podium or wearing their sunglasses!

Motorcycle: Yamaha YZR-M1
Number of MotoGP™ race wins: 84
Number of MotoGP™ World Titles: 7

Crew chief: Silvano Galbusera

Nickname:
The Doctor (he is also known as the GOAT – or Greatest of All Time!)

Race Number: #46
Even though he has won the championship title many times, Vale has never chosen to race the #1 plate on his bike – instead he always keeps his original lucky number 46.

Famous for:
Valentino is very superstitious and has a number of rituals he has to perform at the race track. Prior to riding he always stops about 2 metres from his bike, bending over and reaching for his boot. Then he'll crouch down by the bike and hold the footpeg, which he says helps him focus on what he is about to do, which is to go out and ride a motorcycle very, very fast.

Jorge Lorenzo ⟫⟫⟫⟫⟫⟫⟫

Team: Movistar Yamaha
Nationality: Spanish
Age: 28

Jorge (pronounced haw-hey) Lorenzo is an amazingly consistent rider and is known for being very, very smooth. He is much admired by the other riders although his cool, calm manner before races means race fans don't warm to him like they do some other riders.

Motorcycle: Yamaha YZR-M1

Number of MotoGP™ race wins: 33

Number of MotoGP™ World Titles: 2 (in 2010 and 2012). He also came 2nd in 2011 and 2013, and third in 2014 so, like we said, Jorge is very, very consistent. Jorge also won the 250cc Championship twice.

Crew Chief: Ramon Forcada

Race Number: #99

Nickname:

Por Fuera. This is Spanish for 'round the outside' – and Jorge earned this nick name in the 125cc class by overtaking Dani Pedrosa and Casey Stoner round the outside in a corner rather than the traditional way to overtake of slipping up the inside.

Famous for:

Planting a flag in each country in which he wins a race. Just after winning, Jorge grabs his own black, white and red flag from friends at the side of the track and places it in the ground, accompanied by cheers from his followers. He once celebrated winning a race in Spain by jumping in a pond – wearing his race leathers and boots!

The World of MotoGP™

The MotoGP riders and teams race all over the world, starting in Qatar in the Middle East in March and finishing in Valencia, Spain in November. The aim is to race at each circuit when the weather is good, so that the spectators can enjoy going to the races. The first race is in Qatar in the Middle East and is held at night under floodlights because it's too hot to race during the day, followed by a trip to America. Then it's on to Europe for six races, then another trip to America, then another four races in Europe, followed by three races in Malaysia, Australia and Japan (called the "fly away" rounds), then it's back to Spain for the final round at Valencia.

Every rider and bike travels thousands of miles every year and the hectic schedule means the teams have to be very organised. Every bike and piece of equipment gets packed up immediately after each race and transported to the next round. The process for this has to be faultless, to make sure nothing ever gets left behind – although rumour has it that Valentino Rossi's bike nearly got lost once!

INDIANAPOLIS
USA: 10

AUSTIN
USA: 2

TERMAS DE RIO HONDO
Argentina: 3

| 1: LOSAIL | 4: JEREZ | 7: CATALUNYA | 10: INDIANAPOLIS | 13: MISANO |

| 2: AUSTIN | 5: LE MANS | 8: TT ASSEN | 11: BRNO | 14: MOTORLAND ARAGÓN |

3: TERMAS DE RIO HONDO | **6: MUGELLO** | **9: SACHSENRING** | **12: SILVERSTONE** | **15: TWIN RING MOTEGI**

MotoGP™

TWIN RING MOTEGI
Japan: 15

SEPANG
Malaysia: 17

LOSAIL
Qatar: 1

PHILLIP ISLAND
Australia: 16

16: PHILLIP ISLAND

TT ASSEN / The Netherlands: 8

SILVERSTONE / UK: 12

SACHSENRING / Germany: 9

BRNO / Czech Republic: 11

LE MANS / France: 5

17: SEPANG

MISANO / San Marino: 13

MUGELLO / Italy: 6

18: COM. VAL.
RICARDO TORMO

MOTORLAND ARAGÓN / Spain: 14

CATALUNYA / Spain: 7

COM. VAL. RICARDO TORMO / Spain: 18

JEREZ / Spain: 4

Dani Pedrosa

Team: Repsol Honda
Nationality: Spanish   **Age:** 30

Dani is tiny – just 5 foot 2 and weighs just over 100 pounds. That means he is very aerodynamic on the bike and, because his bike only has a little rider to carry, sometimes he is quicker. There's a downside to being smaller, muscling a MotoGP bike around a track at really fast speeds is hard work and Dani often gets injured and despite his often good race starts, sometimes loses places towards the end of a race.

Motorcycle: Honda RC213V

Number of MotoGP™ race wins: 26

Number of MotoGP™ World Titles: 0.
Dani won the 125cc class in 2003 and then won the 250cc class twice, in 2004 and 2005, so he was a World Champion for three years. Great things were expected of him when he moved to MotoGP, but he has yet to win the title. He can do it – he just needs to beat Valentino Rossi, Jorge Lorenzo and Marc Marquez in every race and that's very, very tough!

Crew chief: Ramon Aurin

Race Number: #26

Nickname:
The Iceman – because Dani very rarely smiles.

Famous for:
Causing a famous crash! Back in 2008 Dani was team mate to American rider Nicky Hayden. Nicky was on the verge of winning the MotoGP Championship title but, in a race, Dani made a mistake, fell off his bike and knocked Nicky off too! He was not very popular that day!

Marc Marquez ⟫⟫⟫

Team: Repsol Honda

Nationality: Spanish

Age: 22

Marc Marquez was the youngest rider ever in history to win MotoGP and amazingly, won it in his very first year on the 1000cc bikes. He is very, very fast, aggressive and determined. Although he always appears happy and smiling, joking with the other riders, he is fiercely competitive and, unlike some other young riders, refuses to let older more experienced riders intimidate him whilst racing.

Motorcycle: Honda RC213V

Number of MotoGP™ race wins: 22

Number of MotoGP™ World Titles: 2. Marc Also won the 125cc title in 2010 and the Moto2 title in 2012

Crew chief: Santi Hernandez

Race Number: #93

Nickname: the Thunder from Cervera (Cervera is where Marc Marquez comes from).

Famous for: Hard work! Marc has made it look easy with his success, but in fact he works very hard. When he was injured, in 2011, and unable to race, he had problems with his eyes and was worried that he would never be able to race again. He was not allowed to ride a bike and had to rest all the time – so he decided to study instead and learned English. Now, when he is interviewed for English TV on the podium, we all understand him.

13

Top Trumps

Who is quickest and where, laptimes and top speeds.

Top Speeds KMH

Rank	Circuit	Rider	Speed	Bike
1	Mugello	Iannone	350.8	Ducati
2	Qatar	Marquez	350.5	Honda
3	Indianapolis	Pedrosa	349	Honda
4	Catalunya	Marquez	347.1	Honda
5	Phillip Island	Marquez	346.2	Honda
6	Austin	Aoyama	344.2	Honda
7	Aragon	Iannone	339	Ducati
8	Valencia	Crutchlow	332.4	Ducati
9	Argentina	Marquez	331.9	Honda
10	Sepang	Dovizioso	329.6	Ducati
11	Silverstone	Dovizioso	328.6	Ducati
12	Assen	Iannone	319.8	Ducati
13	Le Mans	Iannone	316.6	Ducati
14	Brno	Pedrosa	312.5	Honda
15	Motegi	Marquez	309.3	Honda
16	Sachsenring	Dovizioso	298.2	Ducati
17	Jerez	Iannone	295.9	Ducati
18	Misano	Espargaro	289.3	Yamaha

How far riders ride

Rider	KM raced	KM in practice sessions
Stefan BRADL	1737.498	7470.333
Valentino ROSSI	2007.264	7464.328
Bradley SMITH	1971.259	7444.531
Alvaro BAUTISTA	1578.057	7394.288
Pol ESPARGARO	1945.796	7327.755
Dani PEDROSA	1971.072	7103.332
Jorge LORENZO	1966.434	6980.361
Marc MARQUEZ	2064.344	6882.786
Scott REDDING	2097.798	6685.194
Andrea IANNONE	1595.067	6670.02
Andrea DOVIZIOSO	2083.434	6609.645
Cal CRUTCHLOW	1376.919	6502.022
Aleix ESPARGARO	1905.595	6228.452

Lap Records

Circuit	Lap Record	Rider	Year	Bike
Qatar	1'53.927	Lorenzo	2008	Yamaha
Austin	2'02.135	Marquez	2015	Honda
Argentina	1'37.683	Marquez	2014	Honda
Jerez	1'37.190	Lorenzo	2014	Yamaha
Le Mans	1'32.042	Marquez	2014	Honda
Mugello	1'46.489	Iannone	2015	Ducati
Catalunya	1'40.893	Pedrosa	2013	Honda
Assen	1'32.627	Rossi	2015	Yamaha
Sachsenring	1'20.336	Marquez	2015	Honda
Indianapolis	1'31.619	Marquez	2014	Honda
Brno	1'55.527	Crutchlow	2013	Yamaha
Silverstone	2'00.691	Marquez	2013	Honda
Misano	1'32.915	Marquez	2013	Honda
Aragon	1'47.187	Marquez	2014	Honda
Motegi	1'44.502	Dovizioso	2014	Ducati
Phillip Island	1'27.899	Lorenzo	2013	Yamaha
Sepang	1'59.751	Marquez	2014	Honda
Valencia	1'30.237	Marquez	2013	Honda

Success by Country

Country	Number of Riders	Points Awarded (mid-way through 2014	Pole Positions (mid-way through 2014)	Race wins (mid-way through 2014)
Spain	8	544	6	6
Italy	7	443	3	3
Great Britain	4	183		
France	2	16		
Colombia	1	32		
Australia	1	12		
Germany	1	9		
United States	1	8		
Ireland	1	7		
Japan	1	5		
San Marino	1	1		
Czech Republic	1			

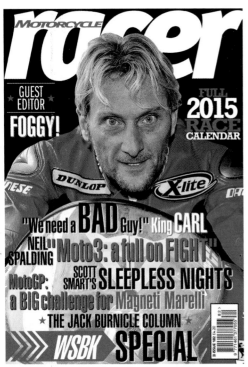

Wordsearch

Can you find the names of the iconic racers, motorcycles, circuits and manufacturers?

```
R R M L O S A I L V G B B K
K A A D T W K P Y A G W X E
E S G V U X L K M L Q O I N
N O N J H C F H S E J L R E
O R E T M T A U H N E H P E
T D T V N N Z T R T L C D H
S E I N F U D A I I C T N S
R P M M K T P H R N Y U A Y
E I A I M S B D L O C R R R
V N R M A D R L Q R R C G R
L A E H T M K M N O O L B A
I D L P L C Z L K S T A G B
S R L F M K X R P S O C T B
F J I M T H G T D I M D G L
```

Motorcycle   Grand Prix   Suzuki

Magneti Marelli   Ducati   Silverstone

Losail   Barry Sheene   Dani Pedrosa

Cal Crutchlow   Valentino Rossi   Aspar

Answers on page 61.

The Race Weekend

MotoGP races usually take place on Sunday afternoon – but the preparations and celebrations mean each race weekend actually starts on Thursday and ends on Monday for the riders, their teams and the people who work behind the scenes in MotoGP.

On Thursday, the trucks that the teams use to carry their equipment arrive at the circuit and park up to form the paddock. Riders arrive in their motorhomes, some of which are really luxurious. The teams are allocated a garage in the pit lane, alongside the track, and start setting up their tools and begin to prepare the bike. The riders have to go to a press conference at tea time, where they answer questions about the race ahead of them.

It's not until Friday that the motorcycles are actually started up and the riders get to ride them around the circuit, but they don't get to ride around all day – instead the times are strictly controlled and the riders have an hour and a half in total to ride their bikes on the track. This time is called Free Practice.

The riders use this time to decide which equipment best suits them and their bike at this particular circuit. They will choose which compound of tyre is best for their bike, which suspension setting they want to use and whether flat-out power or steering through the corner is more important. So, if the rider crashes during this session, or the bike breaks down, the team will not be happy.

On Saturday morning there is another Free Practice session on the track. All the riders want to set a fast time in this session because the top 10 fastest riders have a much easier time on Saturday afternoon, when Qualifying begins.

Qualifying

Qualifying is the system that decides who will start the race at the front of the grid. For safety, everyone doesn't just start the race at the same place on the track. So, the fastest riders start at the front, in rows of three bikes which means they get a head start on the other riders when the race begins.

Free Practice

The slowest riders compete in a session called Qualifying 1 to see who can set the fastest lap in 15 minutes. The quickest two get to join the top ten riders in Qualifying 2 which again is a 15 minute competition to set the fastest lap. These sessions can be really exciting, sometimes more exciting than the race because the riders are put under a lot of pressure and go as fast as they can – even though they don't get prizes for qualifying well!

There is another press conference after Qualifying, and then the riders will talk to their teams about the bike and decide if they want to change any aspect of the settings on the bike before the race on Sunday. Finally, they go to bed – there are no late night parties before race day!

Checking Bike

Post Ride

On Sunday morning all the riders and teams arrive at their garage and get ready for the morning Warm Up session. This allows each team to try out any changes they've made on Saturday evening and see if it's made their bike faster or slower.

Sunday lunchtime (although the riders won't eat a big Sunday lunch before the race) and, at last, it's time for the race to begin. First, every team goes onto their position on the starting grid, with the rider and the bike. You will see many teams have a lady carrying an umbrella to protect the rider from the sun (or the rain) while everyone waits for the race to start. A special tool called a Tyre Warmer is fitted to each tyre on each bike. This warms up the rubber of the tyre so that when the rider begins the race, the tyre can 'stick' to the tarmac on the surface of the track.

Then the riders are allowed one warm up lap around the circuit and then the race begins. The race start is very important – and very dangerous. It is easy to crash because the motorcycles are all very close together, and it is also easy to get overtaken by more aggressive riders, especially if you make a mistake.

The race usually lasts for 45 minutes and once it is over the riders return to their garage talk to their team about the race, and then the job of packing everything up ready for the next round begins. However, the top three riders have to take their motorcycles to 'parc ferme' (which is French for closed area) where they are congratulated by their teams. Then they go onto the podium, receive their trophies and spray some champagne. Then they must do another press conference and then they have lots of journalists queueing up to interview them. They are so busy at this point, and so many people want to talk to them that there are people whose job it is to decide who they should speak to and organise them all, so that the rider does not have to stay talking all night.

Finally, they are allowed to go back to their motorhome and everybody starts to get ready for the next race weekend.

Podium

Warm Up

Yamaha YZR-M1

The YZR-M1 (the M stands for Mission) was first raced in 2002 and has been developed ever since, improving the handling of the bike and making changes to the engine so that the bike could fire out of corners quickly.

YZR-M1 Specs	
Engine	1000cc Liquid cooled inline four-cylinder with crossplane crankshaft
Chassis	Aluminium twin tube delta box with multi-adjustable steering geometry and aluminium swingarm
Top Speed	In excess of 360 km/h (224 mph)
Transmission	Six-speed cassette-type gearbox with alternative gear ratios available
Wheels	MFR Forged Magnesium 16.5″ front, 16.5″ rear
Brakes	Brembo, two 320mm carbon front discs, two four-piston calipers. Single stainless steel rear disc, twin-piston caliper
Power	Over 240 horsepower - 176KW
Suspension	Ohlins upside down front forks and Ohlins rear shock, all adjustable for pre-load and compression rebound damping
Tyres	Bridgestone, 16.5″ front, 16.5″ rear, available as slick and wet tyres
Weight	158 kg
Fuel Allowance	20 litres per race

The Factory Honda RCV213V

The Honda is a very, very fast bike and the two places on the Factory team are highly coveted by all the riders in MotoGP. The Ducati may just beat the RCV213V on outright speed in a straight line but it is built to handle beautifully which is why it holds the lap records at 11 of the 18 GP race circuits.

Honda first raced in Grand Prix in the 1960s and have won the overall title 7 times since the year 2000 (Yamaha have won 6, Ducati 1 and Suzuki 1) and there is always a battle between the top Honda and Yamaha riders as a result.

RC213V Specs	
Dimensions LxWxH	2052mm x 645mm x 1110mm
Wheelbase (mm)	1435mm
Road clearance (mm)	115mm
Weight	As per FIM regulations
Engine type	Liquid-cooled, four-stroke, DOHC 4 valve, V-4
Displacement (cc)	1000cc
Maximum power	Over 175 KW
Frame type	Aluminum twin-tube
Wheels	Front: 16.5" inch Rear: 16.5" inch
Suspension	Front : Telescopic fork / Rear : Pro-link
Fuel tank capacity	20 Litres

Crossword

Test your knowledge of MotoGP in this crossword. If you complete it, you deserve a place on the podium!

Across

1. If a rider sees this they know they've been disqualified.
4. Where on the podium does the race winner get to stand?
6. Who makes the tyres for MotoGP bikes?
8. Which manufacturer did Marco Melandri ride for in 2015?
9. What do teams use to give their riders signals during the race?
11. Which circuit has a corner called The Corkscrew?
13. What protects a rider's eyes whilst racing?
14. How do riders go faster?
16. Which British rider won three races in a row in Moto3 in 2015?
17. What are riders race suits made from?
18. How many cylinders does a MotoGP motorcycle engine have?
19. What do Ohlins, WP and Showa make?
20. What material is used to make the brakes for a MotoGP bike?
21. What's the most important thing to riders?
22. What is the surname of the riders who are brothers in MotoGP?
23. Which circuit hosts the Italian MotoGP round?

Down

2. What do the riders call the on-track sessions that happen before qualifying?
3. Who won the Manufacturer's title in 2014?
5. Which rider won the MotoGP title for Ducati in 2007?
7. What decides riders' starting positions for each race?
10. What helps a rider manage the power of the bike?
12. In what country of the world is the Sepang race circuit?
15. What do you call the men and women at the side of the track that help the riders when they crash?

Answers on page 61.

talent too! To achieve it, he qualified on pole nine times that year and netted 334 points - two more "rookie" records.

And there's more. Marc is only the third Spaniard to win the MotoGP crown. The other Spanish riders who have done this are Jorge Lorenzo who won in 2010 and 2012, and a rider called Alex Criville who won in 1999.

And another incredible fact: MotoGP has existed for nearly 70 years, but in all that time only four riders have won in three categories of racing. Guess what? Marc Marquez is one of those very special four riders. The others are Mike Hailwood, British rider Phil Read and Valentino Rossi. Marc won the 125cc Championship in 2010, Moto2 in 2012 and MotoGP in 2013 so he won three world titles in three classes in a remarkable four years!

His younger brother Alex has bags of talent too; he won the Moto3 class in 2014 and made a strong debut in Moto2 in 2015, so Marc needs to watch out for his younger brother, as he may be challenging him in MotoGP soon.

Marc Marquez won the 2012 Moto2 Championship and in 2013 he began riding in MotoGP as Dani Pedrosa's team mate. Amazingly he finished on the podium in his very first MotoGP race, just being beaten by Valentino Rossi. At his second race, in Texas, he took pole position and won his first race. That achievement earned him a World record, as the youngest ever pole-sitter and race winner in MotoGP (a record set by an American rider called Freddie Spencer back in 1982). He collided with Jorge Lorenzo at Jerez and grabbed second place, then overtook Valentino Rossi on the famous Corkscrew at Laguna Seca, America. He had two immaculate race meetings at Indianapolis and Sachsenring, setting pole, putting in the fastest lap and taking the race win.

It looked like he would win the title before the last race of the season, but he crashed out of second place in Japan and was disqualified for not making a mandatory bike change at Phillip Island (he made a mistake counting the laps!) That meant everything came down to the final race of the year at Valencia; he took third place there and that was enough for him to clinch the title.

He stole another of Freddie Spencer's records – the youngest ever MotoGP Champion and was the first "rookie" to win the title for 35 years. It's a very rare thing to win the title in your first year in MotoGP and requires hard work, total commitment – and

>> Andrea Dovizioso >>>

Team: Ducati

Nationality: Italian

Age: 29

Andrea has been riding in the GP class since 2008 – a long, long time. So he has a lot of experience and skills, but has not had the chance to ride really top factory bikes. Now that Ducati has improved we expect him to be challenging for the title.

Motorcycle: Ducati Desmosedici GP15

Number of MotoGP™ race wins: 1

Number of MotoGP™ World Titles: 0 Dovi did win the 125cc class back in 2004 and he has got 24 podiums in GP!

Race Number: #04

Nickname: Dovi

Crew Chief: Christian Pupulin

Famous for: Sticking with the Ducati team, even when they had big, big problems with their motorcycle. He helped them improve it and develop it and he can now reap the rewards for being patient and loyal. We also think that, because he is Italian, he likes working with an Italian bike manufacturer like Ducati.

>> Andrea Iannone >>>>>>>

Team: Ducati
Yes, two riders called Andrea, in the same team. It must get very confusing in their garage before races.

Nationality: Italian

Age: 26

Andrea Iannone raced in the World 125cc class as early as 2005 and started on 1000cc bikes in 2013. He started off with Ducati and still rides Ducati, and has consistently improved every year, from being in the top 10 in 2013, the top 5 in 2014 and then a 2nd place in the Italian race in 2015.

Motorcycle: Desmosedici GP15

Number of MotoGP™ race wins: 0

Number of MotoGP™ World Titles: 0

Race Number: #29

Nickname: Crazy Joe or The Maniac – both earned from his aggressive and exciting riding style

Crew Chief: Marco Rigamonti

Famous for: Breaking his shoulder in 2015 and going on to race a day or so later in France and then in Italy – and coming second – while in a LOT of pain.

Rider Profiles

》Danilo Petrucci 》》》

Team: Octo Pramac Racing

Nationality: Italian

Age: 25

Danilo started as a test rider for Ducati, then got his break and a ride in Grand Prix in 2012 – he has been quick and impressed lots of people even though he has not been in the GP paddock for as long as other riders.

Motorcycle: Desmosedici GP14.2

Race Number: #9

Best Finish: 8th

Crew chief: Daniele Romagnoli

》Yonny Hernandez 》》》

Team: Octo Pramac Racing

Nationality: Colombian

Age: 27

Motorcycle: Desmosedici GP14.2

Best Finish: 7th

Race Number: #68

Crew chief: Giacomo Guidotti

Famous for: Being the first man from Colombia ever to score points in a Grand Prix race.

Maze: Get to the Grid

Can you help Valentino Rossi get from his motorhome to the grid in time for the race?

1. Motorhome Park

Where the riders all park their motorhomes, where they rest when they are not out on track or being interviewed.

2. Scrutineering

Where the bikes have to be inspected technically before the race, for safety and to make sure the race teams are obeying all the rules.

3. Medical Centre

Where riders go for treatment if they crash.

4. Parc Ferme

Where the top three riders go after the race.

5. Media Centre

Where riders go to be interviewed for the newspapers and magazines that cover MotoGP.

6. Helmet truck

Where the rider takes their helmet for repairs and a new visor before the race.

7. The Team Truck

The huge truck that carries all the team equipment from one race meeting to the next. When it arrives at the circuit, it is parked right next to the team garage so that it's just a few steps away from the garage door.

8. Garage

Where the race team prepare the bike.

9. Pit lane

The road that goes from the garage door to the actual race track.

10. Starting grid

Answer on page 61.

What could possibly go wrong?

Motorcycling racing is dangerous and there's a lot that can go wrong, so of course everyone, from the race organisers to the people who polish the bikes, make safety a top priority.

Riders are usually good at coming up with excuses if they don't do as well in a race as they were expecting to! Sometimes they will blame another racer for riding dangerously and at other times they may say they had 'a technical issue' with their bike. Sometimes it's true!

Which of these do you think has actually happened in a real race?

a. "I ran out of fuel on the very last lap of the race."

b. "I counted the number of laps wrong – I thought we'd finished the race, so I stopped racing – and then found out I had another lap to go!"

c. "I chose the wrong tyre."

d. "Another rider leant over and pressed my kill switch (which stops the engine) at the end of the practice session."

e. "I didn't remember how fast this bike was."

f. "The start was very fast and I got caught off guard."

g. "We are not perfect; we are only human and sometimes we make mistakes. The tyres were different to last year and the temperature of the tarmac was a little colder. I didn't take these circumstances into account."

h. "A bird hit my bike."

i. "I found a dog on the track."

Answers on page 61.

And finally Alvaro Bautista famously celebrated a third place finish at Brno in 2009 by doing a wheelie (riding the bike just on the back wheel) to impress the crowds.

Sadly, it all went wrong for him when the bike flipped too far back, spat him off and sent him sliding along the tarmac on his backside, causing lots of expensive damage to the bike.

Caught on Camera
MotoGP™ 2015, Exciting or What?

Yes, they're touching! Rossi tries to get the inside line on Andrea Dovizioso.

Valentino Rossi wows the Argentinian crowd by saluting Maradona, a footballing national hero.

Oops! Is Yonny Hernandez showing off or crashing?

A Ducati looks just as impressive on one wheel as it does on two – or that's what Andrea Dovizioso thinks.

Anyone fancy a burger? Another use for a Ducati – as a BBQ!!

It's good to be back...Suzuki demonstrate the art of formation flying.

Valentino Rossi and Marc Marquez fighting over the same bit of tarmac...

...Marc wins the battle for the tarmac, but Valentino – amazingly – won the race!

))Pol Espargaro)))

Team: Monster Yamaha Tech 3

Nationality: Spanish

Age: 24

Pol Espargaro won the Moto2 Championship in 2013 and then moved to MotoGP in 2014. He's clever, fast, young and like Marc Marquez, has learned how to ride and how to win in the Moto2 class. That has given both riders an aggressive riding style; they are less worried about riding smoothly and more concerned about riding fast.

Motorcycle: Yamaha YZR-M1

Number of MotoGP™ race wins: 0

Number of MotoGP™ World Titles: 0

Race Number: #44

Nickname: Polyccio

Crew Chief: Nicolas Goyon

Famous for: Being the youngest ever rider to score points in a World Championship race (in the 125cc class in 2006).

))Bradley Smith))))))))

Team: Monster Yamaha Tech 3

Nationality: British

Age: 26

Unlike many British riders in MotoGP, Bradley has competed in Grand Prix for many years. He started in 125cc races in 2006 and won three races in his time on the "little bikes". He moved to Moto2 in the very first year it was run and rode a brand new bike developed by a Frenchman, Guy Coulon from the Tech3 MotoGP team. Bradley never won a race on Guy's bike, but he impressed him enough to get a ride on his MotoGP bike. Bradley has stayed with the team ever since.

Motorcycle: Yamaha YZR-M1

Number of MotoGP™ race wins: 0

Number of MotoGP™ World Titles: 0

Race Number: #38

Crew chief: Guy Coulon

Famous for: Talking! If you ask Bradley a question, be prepared for a long and detailed answer!

Rider Profiles

>>Aleix Espargaro>>>

Team: Suzuki Ecstar

Nationality: Spanish

Age: 26

Motorcycle: Suzuki GSX-RR

Number of MotoGP™ race wins: 0

Number of MotoGP™ World Titles: 0

Race Number: #41

Nickname: Pippo

Famous for: Being the brother of rider Pol Espargaro and the top rider of the non-Factory spec bikes in 2012, 2013 and 2014! He now has a proper Factory bike, the Suzuki, and spent 2015 getting up to speed with it.

>Maverick Vinales>>>>>>

Team: Suzuki Ecstar

Nationality: Spanish

Age: 20

Motorcycle: Suzuki GSX-RR

Number of MotoGP™ race wins: 0

Number of MotoGP™ World Titles: 0

Race Number: #25

Nickname: The Boar

Famous for: Winning Moto3 in 2013 in a battle with a rider named Alex Rins on the last lap of the very last race of the year!

The Bikes

Ducati Desmosedici

The Ducati MotoGP machine has always had a very powerful engine and was able go very fast in a straight line, but was harder to ride around corners than other bikes, which earned it a reputation amongst the riders as being difficult. Australian rider Casey Stoner won the MotoGP title on the Ducati in 2007 and the Ducati was seen by many people as being "Casey's bike" – because no one else could ride it fast enough! Even Valentino Rossi couldn't ride it like Casey did.

In 2014 and 2015 Ducati spent a lot of money to get good people to work on the design of the bike and make it easier to ride and it worked. The Ducati was on the podium in 2015 at almost every race and its two Italian riders Andrea Dovizioso and Andrea Iannone at last showed that Ducati can make a good MotoGP bike.

Ducati Desmosedici Specs	
Engine	Liquid-cooled, 90° V4, four-stroke, evo desmodromic DOHC, four valves per cylinder.
Capacity	1,000cc
Maximum power	Over 240hp
Maximum speed	Over 340 km/h (211mph)
Transmission	Ducati Seamless Transmission (DST). Chain final drive
Carburation	Indirect electronic injection, four throttle bodies with injectors above and below the butterfly valves. Throttles operated by the new EVO 2 TCF (Throttle Control &Feedback) system.
Fuel	Shell Racing V-Power
Lubricant	Shell Advance Ultra 4
Exhaust	Akrapovič
Final Drive	D.I.D Chain
Frame	Aluminum alloy twin-spar
Suspension	Öhlins inverted 48mm front fork and Öhlins rear shock absorber, adjustable for preload, new factory evolution damping system.
Electronics	Magneti Marelli ECU programmed with Ducati factory software
Tyres	Bridgestone 16.5″ front & rear
Brakes	Brembo, two 320mm/340mm carbon front discs with four-piston callipers. Single stainless steel rear disc with two-piston calliper
Dry weight	158kg (348 lbs.)

Suzuki GSX-RR

Suzuki GSX-RR Specs	
Dimensions LxWxH	2,096mm x 720mm x 1,140mm
Wheelbase (mm)	1,457mm
Engine	Water-cooled, four-stroke in-line four-cylinder, DOHC four-valve
Displacement	1,000cm3
Maximum output	Over 169kw (230PS)
Maximum speed	Over 330km/h
Gearbox	Six-speed (cassette type)
Frame type	Twin-spar Aluminum
Tyres (front/ rear)	16.5″/16.5″
Front suspension	Öhlins, inverted fork
Rear suspension	Öhlins
Brakes	Carbon disk/ steel disk, Brembo

Suzuki pulled out of MotoGP racing in 2011 after an earthquake made business life difficult in Japan; where the company is based. However, the engineers at Suzuki never stopped thinking about racing and worked on a bike, the GSX-RR, and brought it to MotoGP at the end of 2014.

Because it is a brand new motorcycle it wasn't expected to race well straight away. Its engine wasn't very powerful to begin with but its handling, or ability to steer its way through corners, was very good. Its riders, Aleix and Maverick, who are both Spanish, actually set pole position and second place on the grid at the race in Barcelona, Spain after only a few races, although they didn't manage to convert that to a win on race day!

>>Stefan Bradl >>>>>>

Team: Aprilia Racing Team Gresini

Nationality: German

Age: 25

Motorcycle: Aprilia RS-GP15

Number of MotoGP™ race wins: 0

Number of MotoGP™ World Titles: 0. Stefan won 2 races in 125cc, 5 Moto2 races and won the Moto2 title in 2011, so he is used to winning. However, he hasn't always been on the most competitive motorcycles since he moved up to the MotoGP class. He swapped from a Yamaha to the Aprilia mid-way through 2015, qualified higher than his teammate Alvaro straight away and is looking forward to developing the new Aprilia even more in 2016.

Race Number: #6

Crew Chief: Diego Gubellini

Famous for: Winning his first race at the Brno circuit in Czech Republic, where his father Helmut Bradl also won a race several years before.

>>Alvaro Bautista >>>>>>>

Team: Aprilia Racing Team Gresini

Nationality: Spanish

Age: 31

Alvaro has been racing in Grand Prix since 2002 and won the 125cc Championship in 2006. He has raced with the big names – Casey Stoner, Jorge Lorenzo and Andrea Dovizioso but has only set pole position once and his best ever result is third place.

Crew chief: Giulio Nava

Nickname: Bati

Race Number: #19

Motorcycle: Aprilia RS-GP15

Rider Profiles

>>Jack Miller >>>>>>>>>>

Team: CWM LCR Honda

Nationality: Australian

Age: 21

Jack Miller's first year in MotoGP was 2015 so he's still very, very new to the class. He started racing in GPs in 2011 when he was only 17; his mother moved all the way from Australia to Germany with him so that he could race at World Championship level so he is under pressure to do well.

Motorcycle: Honda RC213V-RS. Although Jack is in the same team as Cal, his bike is of a lower specification, which is fair enough as Jack is a 'rookie'.

Number of MotoGP™ race wins: 0

Number of MotoGP™ World Titles: 0. Jack very nearly won the Moto3 title in 2014 when he rode on a KTM Motorcycle

Race Number: #43

Crew Chief: Cristian Gabarrini

Nickname: Jackass

Famous for: Jack is the only rider ever to move straight from the Moto3 class to MotoGP – usually racers compete in Moto2 (on "medium-sized bikes") before getting onto the incredibly fast 1000cc machines. All the Moto3 riders watched Jack carefully at first, because if he did well, they believed they could go straight to MotoGP too.

>>Cal Crutchlow>>>

Team: CWM LCR Honda

Nationality: British

Age: 31

Cal started in MotoGP in 2011 with the Tech3 team (who Bradley Smith now rides for) then he rode the Ducati and now he has a very good Honda motorcycle; not quite as good as Marc Marquez's and Dani Pedrosa's bikes but not too different. So, unlike many other riders, Cal has ridden three different motorcycles in three years and has had to adapt how he rides and learn about each one of them. That means we haven't seen the best of Cal Crutchlow yet and we expect great things of him in 2016.

Motorcycle: Honda RC213V

Number of MotoGP™ race wins: Cal hasn't won a race yet, but he has qualified fastest twice and has finished second in a race.

Number of MotoGP™ World Titles: 0. Unlike many of his rivals, Cal has not won a 125, 250 or Moto2 title either – because he never raced in those championships! Instead he was busy becoming British Supersport Champion and then competed in World Superbikes before moving to MotoGP.

Race Number: #35

Crew Chief: Christophe 'Beefy' Bourgignon

Nickname: the Dog

Famous for: Cycling. Cal's favourite sport involves cycling for many miles, including some very steep hills. He enjoys it and it's an essential part of his very strict fitness regime. We believe he could become a professional cyclist if he ever wanted to leave motorcycling. Cal is also a Manchester United fan.

Aprilia RS-GP

Aprilia is an Italian motorcycle manufacturer and the company has been involved in racing for many years. Aprilia dominated the 125cc and 250cc classes before they were replaced with Moto3 and Moto2 and most former MotoGP World Champions have raced Aprilias.

Aprilia only started racing in MotoGP fully in 2015 (before that they did supply engines to a couple of race teams). Their plan was actually to start in 2016 but the boss decided he couldn't wait that long.

The RS-GP has some things in common with the Aprilia RSV4, a motorcycle that you can buy to ride on the road and which won the Superbike World Championship in 2014. The team is constantly developing the bike, trying to improve the power and the handling so the riders have to be very patient and must accept that they won't win races just yet.

Aprilia Racing RS-GP Specs	
Engine	Aprilia V4
Power	255 BHP
Top speed	350km/h
Gearbox	6 speed cassette gearbox
Suspension	Ohlins
Chassis	Aluminium
Brakes	Brembo
Fuel allowance	24L
Software	Aprilia Racing
Dry weight	160 Kg

The Open Class Honda RC213V-RS

The people who organise MotoGP want to have lots of motorcycles on the grid at the start of each race, because it makes the racing more exciting to watch. But racing is expensive and not many people can afford to run a MotoGP race team, let alone build one of the fastest motorcycles in the world. So, the organisers encouraged Honda to make a motorcycle that other teams could buy and race. The result is the RC213V-RS, also known as the "production Honda" which is very similar to the Factory Honda, but it has a less sophisticated gear box and more standard electronics. That's because Honda don't want other teams to beat their own Factory riders!

RC213V-RS Specs	
Dimensions LxWxH	2,096mm x 720mm x 1,140mm
Wheelbase	1.435 mm
Weight	160 kg
Engine	Liquid cooled, four-stroke, DOHC 4 valve, V-4
Displacement	1000cc
Maximum power	Over 192 KW (over 250 hp)
Top speed	Over 350 Km/h
Gearbox	Six speed cassette type gearbox with alternative optional ratio
Clutch	Fully adjustable multi plate slipper clutch
Suspension	Front: Fully adjustable Öhlins TRVSP25 diam 48mm upside down
	Rear: Fully adjustable Öhlins TRSP44
Brakes	Front: Brembo 4 pistons caliper, 320/340mm Brembo carbon disc
	Rear: Brembo Twin piston caliper, 196mm Yutaka steel disc
Tyres	Front and rear 16.5"
Chassis	Aluminium twin spar frame fully adjustable steering and geometry. Fully adjustable HRC magnesium triple clamp
Fuel tank capacity	24 litres

Behind the Scenes: The People

When a race is underway, everybody focuses on the riders on the track and there are up to 30 of them in one race. However, MotoGP involves a lot more people who work behind the scenes to make sure the races can take place.

At each circuit there are medical staff and marshals to look after the riders if there is an accident. You might see these people at work if there is a crash during the race. There are thousands of other people at work who you won't see, for example, the people who feed the medics, marshals, race officials, riders and teams. Can you think of other jobs at the circuit that must need doing during a race meeting?

Timing 〉

It's usually pretty easy to tell who is in the lead in a race, but the timing, the time it takes a rider to complete an entire lap and individual sections of the track (called sectors) is very important to the rider and to their team. It allows them to see where they are going fast and where they are going slowly, compared to their competitors and that allows them to understand where they can improve. Obviously, it's also important at the end of race to know who came first, second and third, but riders want to know exactly where they came, even those in last place, and exactly how long it took them to complete each lap. So the people who run the timing systems are crucial to the success of every track session.

Mechanics and team managers sometimes get interviewed by the television crews who cover MotoGP but a race team involves a lot of other people as well – there are people who construct the hospitality units where teams entertain the sponsors who pay for them to go racing, and the public relations people who organise interviews between newspaper journalists, the riders and team managers. Even further behind the scenes we have the people who organise each race. Next time you see a race on television, watch what happens when the top three riders come into pit lane. You will see men and women moving the riders from place to place, from their bike to the journalists and then to the podium.

At each race meeting the teams will need tyres, motorcycle parts and rider equipment, and all of these items have to be available at the circuit. So, the companies that make these things will send spares and people to the race track to make sure the riders and teams have exactly what they need just when they need it – sometimes in the middle of the night, if the team is working on the motorcycle to get it ready for the next day's race.

It looks very cool to wear a pass around your neck that allows you to access all areas at a race meeting (pit lane, the team garages and so on), but trust me; the people who wear these passes are very special and work very hard to make sure every MotoGP is a success.

Racing in the Rain

falling while they race, every corner of every lap can be different. That means you will see more crashes than normal.

So, the riders must be careful and most importantly, use less power than they normally would. That's very good news for riders on less powerful bikes. In a wet race they can often catch up with the faster riders and if they avoid mistakes and don't slide off the track they can be on the podium, whereas usually they would be back in tenth place.

The rider isn't the only factor, although he's a very important one, in rainy weather. Racing on wet tarmac requires different tyres to the normal 'slicks'. Wet weather tyres or 'wets' as they are called have treaded patterns cut into them that divert the water away from the centre of the tyre so that it can stick onto the track better. Wets are also made of softer rubber, so that they warm up quicker and give more grip even when it's cold and wet. The downside is that if 'wets' are used on a hot, dry track they wear out very, very quickly.

If you've ever ridden your own bike when it's raining, you'll know it's not much fun – and it's more difficult because your tyres are more likely to slip. Most MotoGP racers don't like racing in the rain but wet weather makes racing very interesting to watch.

Racing in the rain requires riders to use great skill. They must judge how fast they can ride and how much they can lean the bike over without slipping and because more rain might be

Spray on the track presents another problem for the riders. Water coming off the back wheel of the bike in front of them appears, limiting what they can see ahead of them. They have to turn on a bright red rear light (like a fog light on a car) in the rain so that other riders can see their bikes, but that doesn't help much. Spray also lands on the visor of their helmet and they ride far too quickly to be able to wipe it off.

If the weather is really bad the race organisers will talk to the riders and teams and between them they will decide if it's actually safe to race. In the past we've seen so many riders fall off during a wet race that there have only just been three riders finishing to go onto the podium at the end of the race. Nobody wants a rider to be injured or a bike to be damaged when it could be avoided so the organisers sometimes have difficult decisions to make.

At the start of a race, the race organisers will decide if a race is 'dry' or 'wet' and the teams will then know which sort of tyres to use. Of course it may start raining unexpectedly once the race has started (especially at the British Grand Prix) but the race will keep going. For that reason, each team will look carefully at the weather forecast before the race and decide if they should use wets or slicks at the start.

If you've ever had to replace the tyre on a bicycle or help fit a new car wheel you will know how hard it can be. MotoGP teams will not change tyres on the bikes during a race. Instead, they have a second motorcycle ready in the garage with wet weather tyres already fitted. If it starts to rain during the race, the rider will come into pit lane and 'hop' on to their second bike and go back out on track to complete the race. This makes for some very entertaining moments in the pit lane, with some riders making a single jump from one bike to the other.

Engine

MotoGP bikes have big powerful engines with up to 1000cc and a maximum of four cylinders. In the past the class has been based around two-stroke 500cc engines and more recently 800cc four-stroke engines. However, in 2012 the rule was changed so that everyone races 1000cc four stroke engines and this makes sense as it's an engine size that is used on many motorcycles built for the road. That means a lot of motorcycle manufacturers already make 1000cc engines and in theory the teams will find it easier and cheaper to buy and develop their engines. In reality, the engines on MotoGP bikes are very, very special and very expensive and aim to deliver as much power as they can.

You might think that the bike with the most powerful engine would automatically go faster than the others and win all the races. In fact the engineers have to look carefully at how long the engines will last as well as how powerful they are. There isn't much point having a really fast engine that blows up after one lap!

The rules actually limit the number of engines a rider can use each year. For the top riders who race for the Factory teams, a maximum of 5 engines may be used and if they blow them all up or break them, and they have to use a sixth engine then they are made to start the race behind all the other riders. New teams and those that haven't been on the podium for a while are allowed 12 engines per rider.

The engine is clearly an important component of the bike, but a good MotoGP needs the highest level of technology to transfer that engine power into making the wheels of the bike go round the race track fast and of course, it needs a skilled rider to race it.

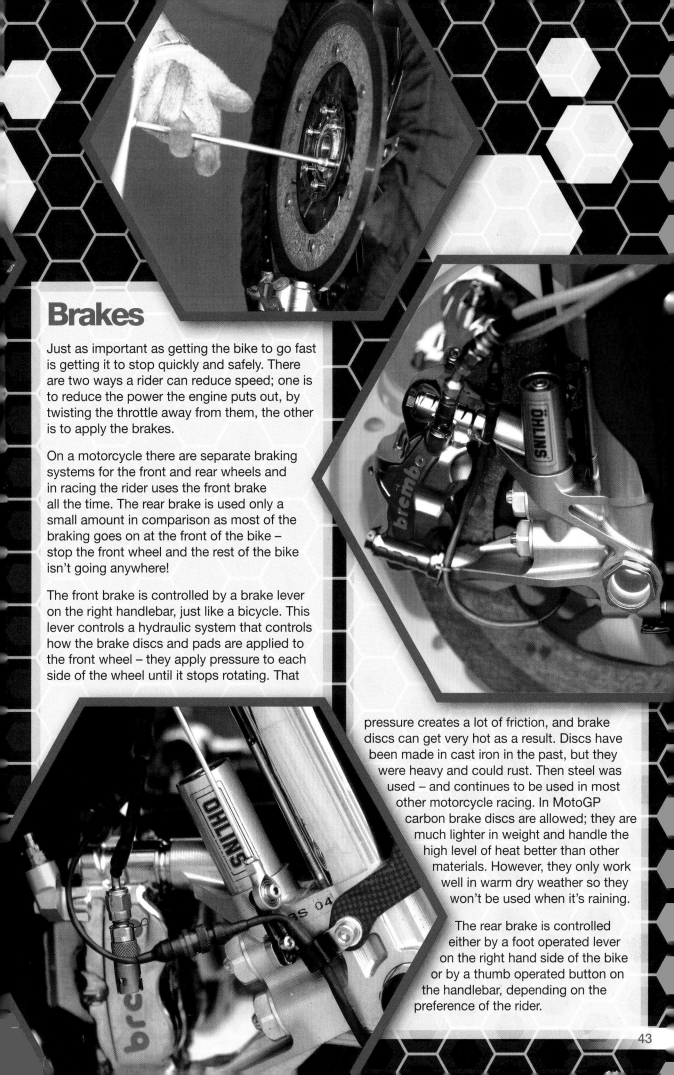

Brakes

Just as important as getting the bike to go fast is getting it to stop quickly and safely. There are two ways a rider can reduce speed; one is to reduce the power the engine puts out, by twisting the throttle away from them, the other is to apply the brakes.

On a motorcycle there are separate braking systems for the front and rear wheels and in racing the rider uses the front brake all the time. The rear brake is used only a small amount in comparison as most of the braking goes on at the front of the bike – stop the front wheel and the rest of the bike isn't going anywhere!

The front brake is controlled by a brake lever on the right handlebar, just like a bicycle. This lever controls a hydraulic system that controls how the brake discs and pads are applied to the front wheel – they apply pressure to each side of the wheel until it stops rotating. That

pressure creates a lot of friction, and brake discs can get very hot as a result. Discs have been made in cast iron in the past, but they were heavy and could rust. Then steel was used – and continues to be used in most other motorcycle racing. In MotoGP carbon brake discs are allowed; they are much lighter in weight and handle the high level of heat better than other materials. However, they only work well in warm dry weather so they won't be used when it's raining.

The rear brake is controlled either by a foot operated lever on the right hand side of the bike or by a thumb operated button on the handlebar, depending on the preference of the rider.

>>> Scott Redding >>>

Team: Estrella Galicia 0,0 Marc VDS

Nationality: British

Age: 22

Motorcycle: Honda RC213V

Best Result in MotoGP™: 7th

Race Number: #45

Crew chief: Chris Pike

Famous for: Being the youngest rider to ever win a Grand Prix. Scott won the 125GP race at Silverstone in June 2008 when he was 15 years old, when most boys his age were taking exams (he still had to do homework between track sessions though). Some people have compared him to Barry Sheene, the most famous British Grand Prix rider ever, so people expect a lot from Scott. Scott is very tall for a racer and because of that he works hard to lose weight so that he doesn't make the bike too slow during races – but he loves pasta!

>>Nicky Hayden>>>>>

Team: Aspar Team MotoGP™

Nationality: American

Age: 34

Motorcycle: Honda RC213V-RS

Number of MotoGP™ race wins: 3

Number of MotoGP™ World Titles: 1

Race Number: #69. Nicky says this is his favourite number because if he crashes and his bike lands upside down, his number will look the same!

Crew chief: Matthew Casey

Nickname: The Kentucky Kid

Famous for: Winning the MotoGP crown back in 2006 for Honda. Unlike many other riders, Nicky didn't race smaller bikes at Grand Prix, like 125s and 250s. Instead, he became the youngest ever American National Champion and then moved straight to riding 1000cc motorcycles at World Championships!

>>Eugene Laverty>>>>>>>

Team: Aspar Team MotoGP™

Nationality: Irish

Age: 29

Eugene hasn't won a world title yet but racing in MotoGP is what he has wanted to do since he was very young. He has come close to winning championships several times. Like Nicky, he hasn't ridden in Grand Prix all his career, apart from racing 250cc GPs in 2007 and 2008 he has raced in British Supersport, World Supersport and World Superbike. 2015 was his first year in GP and it was the Aspar team's first year with the Honda.

Motorcycle: Honda RC213V-RS

Number of MotoGP™ race wins: 0

Number of MotoGP™ World Titles: 0

Race Number: #50

Crew Chief: Andrea Orlandi

Nickname: Norge

Tyres

Tyres play a crucial role in MotoGP – as they do on any motorcycle. They are the final piece of the jigsaw as they help the bike connect or "grip" to the tarmac.

In racing you will hear a lot of talk about tyres. People might say, for example, "Valentino Rossi has looked after his tyres well". That does not mean he sat in his garage cleaning them! It means he has ridden in a way that ensures that his tyres will work well for him and provide grip all the way through the race, from the first lap through to the very last, and not be worn out.

If a rider accelerates hard, brakes hard, stops or starts and rides in a jerky way, which is typically what happens if they need to overtake other riders or if they are just riding as fast as they possibly can, then their tyres will wear out quicker.

It's a bit like eating an ice cream– too cold and it's hard to eat, too hot and it melts and drips; somewhere in the middle, it will be "just right" and it's a similar situation with race tyres.

Grip happens when the rubber makes contact with the tarmac; when it is the right temperature part of it will melt onto the tarmac that makes the bike 'stick'. But part of the tyre will be left on the track and the rider won't be able to use it again. (Imagine the rubber of the tyre is like chewing gum!). The stickier the rubber is, the more able the bike is to grip the tarmac and the rider is able to go faster and lean the bike over more without crashing. But if the tyre wears, it becomes unable to grip, and the rider is more likely to lose control and fall off.

All the tyres that the riders use are the same size and they are all made by the same company, Michelin. This is to make sure that the racing is fair. In the past, tyre companies would make a special tyre just for one rider, to work on just their bike for one weekend only, sometimes making it on the Saturday night before the race and delivering it just in time for Sunday! This was very expensive and only the richest teams could afford it, so it was perhaps a little bit unfair, because tyres do make a big difference to the speeds and lap times riders can do. Now, although everyone races on Michelins, the tyres are not all the same! They all look the same, they are black and round, but they can work very differently. You will hear people refer to hard tyres and soft tyres. Soft tyres get hot and stick to the tarmac quicker, but they wear out quicker. Hard tyres give less adhesion to the circuit, but will last longer and tend to be able to grip better towards the end of a race.

How do a rider and his team choose the correct tyre? It varies according to a number of things. Firstly, the weather. When it is hot, a soft tyre will wear slightly more quickly. Secondly, the circuit. Think of a circuit that has just four left hand corners; the rider will use a lot of rubber on the left hand side of the tyre when they lean the bike over into the corners, but the right hand side of the tyre will not make contact with the tarmac at all. The people who make the tyres have to think about all these things when deciding which tyres they must give to the teams and work all year round to make new tyres and to try new ideas.

Electronics

You won't see computer programmers at MotoGP much, but they play an important role in racing because they write the software for the electronic systems for the motorcycles. Every motorcycle will have a little black box fitted to it. This box is made by an Italian company called Magneti Marelli and everybody uses the same electronics to ensure fair racing.

If you are cycling and want to go quicker, you peddle harder and you might change gear. Imagine something was controlling how much quicker you could go, regardless of how hard you peddled! That's what

electronics do. For that reason, some riders don't like to have the electronics interfering too much, whilst others use all the electronics they can. Riders can choose how much or how little electronic control is available – they can even change it during the race, whilst they are riding along!

If the engine is the 'heart' of the bike and the tyres are the 'shoes', the electronics are its brain. They help to keep the riders safe and the bikes more controllable so, when the rider opens the throttle to go faster, to make the engine rev faster and make the rear wheel turn faster, the electronics control how quickly that process happens.

You may hear people talk about electronic 'maps'. A map is just a group of settings that the rider and the team decide on to get the very best from their bike. For example, when a rider accelerates out of a corner, the front wheel can feel lighter to the rider and start to rise up in the air (called a wheelie). Anti-wheelie control can be programmed into the bike to prevent this effect, by deciding how much power to feed to the back wheel and how quickly this happens.

If a rider is turning into or coming out of a corner it is especially important. Too much power and the bike will slide. The rider, of course, knows this but the electronics can be programmed to decide exactly when to deliver the power – and when not to! All this helps to keep the rider safe.

>>Claudio Corti>>>>>>>>>>

Team: Forward Racing

Nationality: Italian

Age: 28

Since 2005 Claudio has raced 1000cc bikes in European Superstock, then he raced in Moto2 and then in MotoGP, then World Superbike and now he is back in MotoGP! So he has a lot of experience riding different motorcycles, but probably needs a couple of years with the same team so that he can focus on his riding.

Motorcycle: Yamaha Forward

Number of MotoGP™ race wins: 0

Number of MotoGP™ World Titles: 0

Race Number: 71

Crew chief: Sergio Verbena

Famous for: Winning the European Superstock 600 Championship in 2005.

>>Loris Baz>>>>>>>

Team: Forward Racing

Nationality: French

Age: 22

Motorcycle: Yamaha Forward

Number of MotoGP™ race wins: 0

Number of MotoGP™ World Titles: 0

Race Number: #76

Nickname: Bazooka

Famous for: Not obeying team orders. 2015 was Loris Baz' first year in MotoGP and before that he rode in World Superbikes as team mate of Britain's Tom Sykes. In 2014 Tom Sykes was close to winning the championship and Loris was told by his team to let Tom beat him to get the most points possible. Loris refused, and Tom lost the title to the Frenchman Sylvain Guintoli!

Rider Profiles

»Mike di Meglio»»

Team: Avintia Racing

Nationality: French

Age: 27

Crew chief: Alessandro Tognelli

Famous for: Winning the 125 World Championship in 2008. He then raced in Moto2 and only moved to MotoGP in 2014, so he's still very new to the big 1000cc bikes.

Race Number: #63

Motorcycle: Desmosedici GP14

Best result: 12th

»Hector Barbera»»»»»»

Team: Avintia Racing

Nationality: Spanish

Age: 29

Motorcycle: Desmosedici GP14

Best result: 5th

Race Number: #8

Crew chief: Jarno Polastri

Nickname: Streisand (after actress Barbara Streisand, just because Hector's last name is a bit like the girl's name!).

Famous for: Breaking his leg in a horrible accident in Motegi, Japan in 2012. Also, the letters of his name also spell "Bathrobe racer".

Frames

The frame of a MotoGP bike is very special and is built for racing and racing alone. Its job is to help the rider use the power of the engine to go fast on the track.

The frames are made from metal alloys (blends of metal and other materials) and you might expect that a very rigid or stiff frame would be the best. Imagine a bicycle frame made of jelly – it would be unrideable. In motorcycle racing you need the frame to flex, so that when the bike turns into the corner and the rider is leaning over, the frame 'gives' a bit, allowing the bike to bend and adapt to the corner. This allows the rider to ride round a corner faster –otherwise they would have to stay more upright or risk crashing the bike.

The engineers who make the bikes analyse which areas of the frame need to bend in a corner and then modify the frame so that it uses less stiff materials in those areas.

Suspension

Suspension is the term given to the system of springs, shock absorbers and linkages that connect a bike to its wheels. Suspension systems serve a dual purpose. They are used whenever the bike turns or the brakes are applied, but also provide some comfort to the rider when they go over a bump by softening the bike's reaction. These two goals are at odds with each other and it's all about finding the right compromise. As a result race teams spend many hours finding the right suspension setup and the best settings will vary depending on who is riding the bike, which race circuit they are at, the weather, the tyres, the gearing – everything!

Imagine braking on a bike that is going really fast. When you brake, the pads around the front wheel make contact with the wheel rims to slow the bike down. On a standard bicycle there is no suspension – instead your arms take the pressure. On a motorcycle because the speeds are so much faster, arms are not enough. Suspension kits work like springs – in fact if you look closely you will see these springs connecting the frame to the rear wheel.

Spring

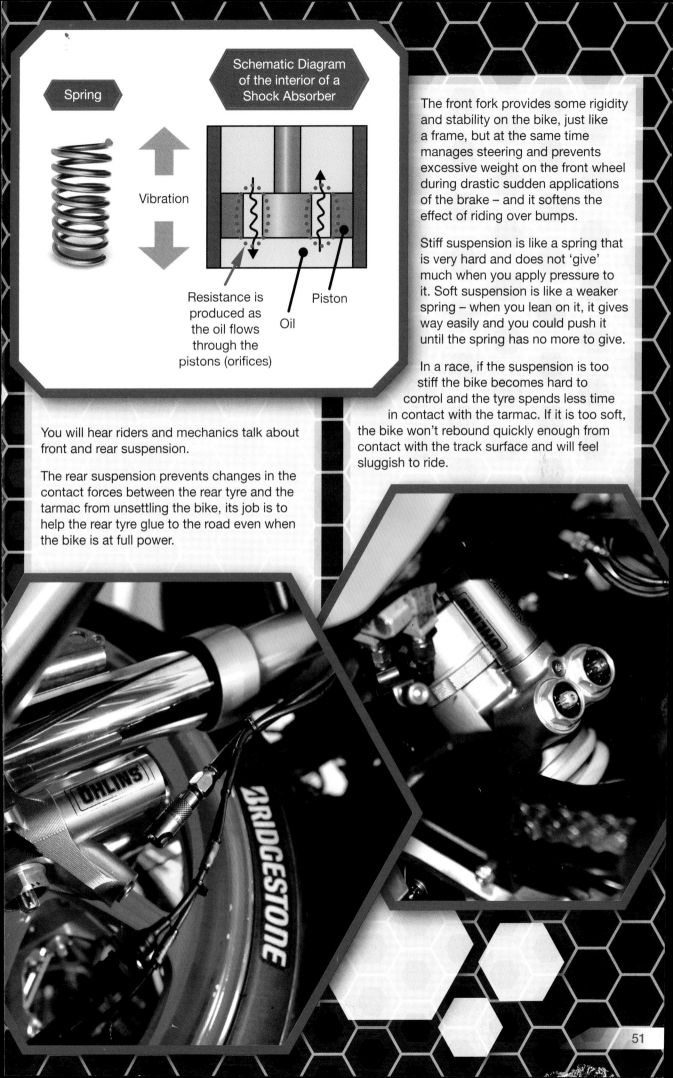

Vibration

Schematic Diagram of the interior of a Shock Absorber

Resistance is produced as the oil flows through the pistons (orifices)

Oil

Piston

The front fork provides some rigidity and stability on the bike, just like a frame, but at the same time manages steering and prevents excessive weight on the front wheel during drastic sudden applications of the brake – and it softens the effect of riding over bumps.

Stiff suspension is like a spring that is very hard and does not 'give' much when you apply pressure to it. Soft suspension is like a weaker spring – when you lean on it, it gives way easily and you could push it until the spring has no more to give.

In a race, if the suspension is too stiff the bike becomes hard to control and the tyre spends less time in contact with the tarmac. If it is too soft, the bike won't rebound quickly enough from contact with the track surface and will feel sluggish to ride.

You will hear riders and mechanics talk about front and rear suspension.

The rear suspension prevents changes in the contact forces between the rear tyre and the tarmac from unsettling the bike, its job is to help the rear tyre glue to the road even when the bike is at full power.

Spot the Difference

There are 5 things different in pictures 1 and 2. Can you spot them?
Check your answers on page 61.

Past Winners

This list of winners over the last 30 years includes the names of many legends from present day heroes to Barry Sheene, the last British rider to win the title.

Year	Rider	Country	Bike
2014	M Marquez	Spain	Honda
2013	M Marquez	Spain	Honda
2012	J Lorenzo	Spain	Yamaha
2011	C Stoner	Australia	Honda
2010	J Lorenzo	Spain	Yamaha
2009	V Rossi	Italy	Yamaha
2008	V Rossi	Italy	Yamaha
2007	C Stoner	Australia	Ducati
2006	N Hayden	America	Honda
2005	V Rossi	Italy	Yamaha
2004	V Rossi	Italy	Yamaha
2003	V Rossi	Italy	Honda
2002	V Rossi	Italy	Honda
2001	V Rossi	Italy	Honda
2000	K Roberts Jr	America	Suzuki
1999	A Criville	Spain	Honda
1998	M Doohan	Australia	Honda
1997	M Doohan	Australia	Honda
1996	M Doohan	Australia	Honda
1995	M Doohan	Australia	Honda
1994	M Doohan	Australia	Honda
1993	K Schwantz	America	Suzuki
1992	W Rainey	America	Yamaha
1991	W Rainey	America	Yamaha
1990	W Rainey	America	Yamaha
1989	E Lawson	America	Honda
1988	E Lawson	America	Yamaha
1987	W Gardner	Australia	Honda
1986	E Lawson	America	Yamaha
1985	F Spencer	America	Honda
1984	E Lawson	America	Yamaha
1983	F Spencer	America	Honda
1982	F Uncini	Italy	Suzuki
1981	M Lucchinelli	Italy	Suzuki
1980	K Roberts	America	Yamaha
1979	K Roberts	America	Yamaha
1978	K Roberts	America	Yamaha
1977	B Sheene	Britain	Suzuki
1976	B Sheene	Britain	Suzuki
1975	G Agostini	Italy	Yamaha

Moto2™

>> Moto2 is right in the middle between Moto3 and MotoGP and there are more than 30 riders on the grid. Every Moto2 race is exciting because the racing is very close and lap times are very similar.

The engines are 600cc in size and unlike MotoGP or Moto3, every single motorcycle has to use an identical engine, which is made by Honda and they are all tuned to exactly the same level. They all have to race using the same make of tyre too, made by Dunlop. The rest of the bike is up to the Moto2 teams; they can buy different frames and suspension and all the other pieces that make a motorcycle.

A few teams make their own frame – for example the Speed Up team and the Tech3 team – but most teams buy a pack including frame, swing arm and other components. The most popular kit to buy is from a German company called Kalex.

The minimum weight limit is 215Kg, so the bike, the rider, their leathers, helmet and boots must weigh at least that.

So, the teams need to make a motorcycle that is fast, yet comfortable and relatively easy for the racer to ride. Every bike has its strong and weak points – some are good at slowing down quickly into the corner, others are better at turning out of the corner and allowing the rider to accelerate quickly. So, it is down to the rider to understand the good points of their bike and ride in a style that uses those good things.

Moto2™ Star: Sam Lowes

>> Sam Lowes is from Lincoln in England and he is a former World Supersport Champion. Unlike many of his competitors he hasn't ever raced in the Moto3 class. Instead he competed in the British Championships, then World Supersport and then in Moto2. He started riding in Moto2 in 2014 and won his first race in 2015, at Austin in Texas.

Sam started racing in 2002 when he was 13. He has an identical twin brother, Alex Lowes, who competes in World Superbike. He and Alex train together and play golf with each other and with fellow racers, and their matches get very, very competitive!

>> Age: 26 >> Weight: 66Kg
>> Height: 168cm (5'6") >> Race Number #22

Valencia

The very special Valencia circuit in Spain always hosts the final MotoGP race of the year and sometimes it's a very tense race because it can be where the overall champions of each of the three races classes are finally decided.

At the end of the weekend, when the races are over, every rider knows exactly where they have finished in the championship, whether they are at the top or the bottom of the points table.

There is a big party on Sunday evening after the races, not just for the riders but for the teams, the organisers and the people who work behind the scenes and the television people as well.

Valencia is very easy to recognize on television or from photographs because of the distinctive yellow building and, because it's in Spain it's usually sunny with a bright blue sky.

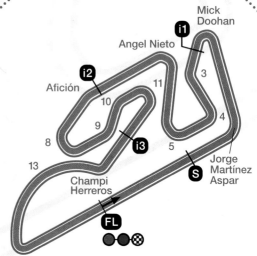

It is also known as the Circuit Ricardo Tormo and was built in 1999 and has been used to host MotoGP races ever since then. It is 2.517 miles in length. Riders like the challenge of the circuit – it's technical and twisty, rather than very fast and has five right handed corners, nine left handers and a 876 metre straight. Although the track is regarded as quite small, the pit complex contains 48 garages whilst the stadium style grandstands can seat up to 150,000 spectators. Spanish rider Dani Pedrosa likes Valencia particularly – he has won here 6 times!

The circuit layout is very clever because wherever spectators sit, they can see all parts of the circuit and everything that happens in the race. This creates a unique atmosphere which is enjoyed by the race fans and also the riders themselves. Because of this, a lot of people come to the Valencia GP race meeting - 197,000 last year!

The next day, when the racing is finished for the year and the party is over, you might expect that everyone goes home and has a break, but no! The very next day, the teams and riders are back at work, starting to prepare and test the bikes for the following year.

Fast Facts

Valencia Lap Record: Marc Marquez, 1m 31.515 seconds during the race. Marc also set a stunning fastest qualifying time here, of 1m 30.237 seconds! The record for the top speed recorded here goes to Britain's Cal Crutchlow who reached an amazing 332.4 kilometers per hour.

Circuit Ricardo Tormo

>>Alex de Angelis >>>>>

Team:
e-motion loda
Racing Team

Nationality:
Sammarinese

Age: 31

Alex has vast experience! He did his first Grand Prix in 1999 and has won races in 250GP and Moto2. He has switched teams, bikes and race series several times and maybe, with the same bike and same team he can start doing well!

Motorcycle: ART GP14

First race: 2008

Best Finish: 2nd

Race Number: #15

Crew chief: Giovanni Sandi

>>Karel Abraham>>>>>>>

Team:
AB Motoracing

Nationality:
Czech

Age: 25

Motorcycle: Honda RC213V-RS

First race: 2011

Best finish: 7th

Race Number: #17

Crew chief: Marco Grana

Nickname: Abaja

Famous for: Unlike many of the riders he races against, Karel has not won a championship, although he did win a Moto2 race in 2010. He has always raced for the Cardion AB team which is owned and funded by his father.

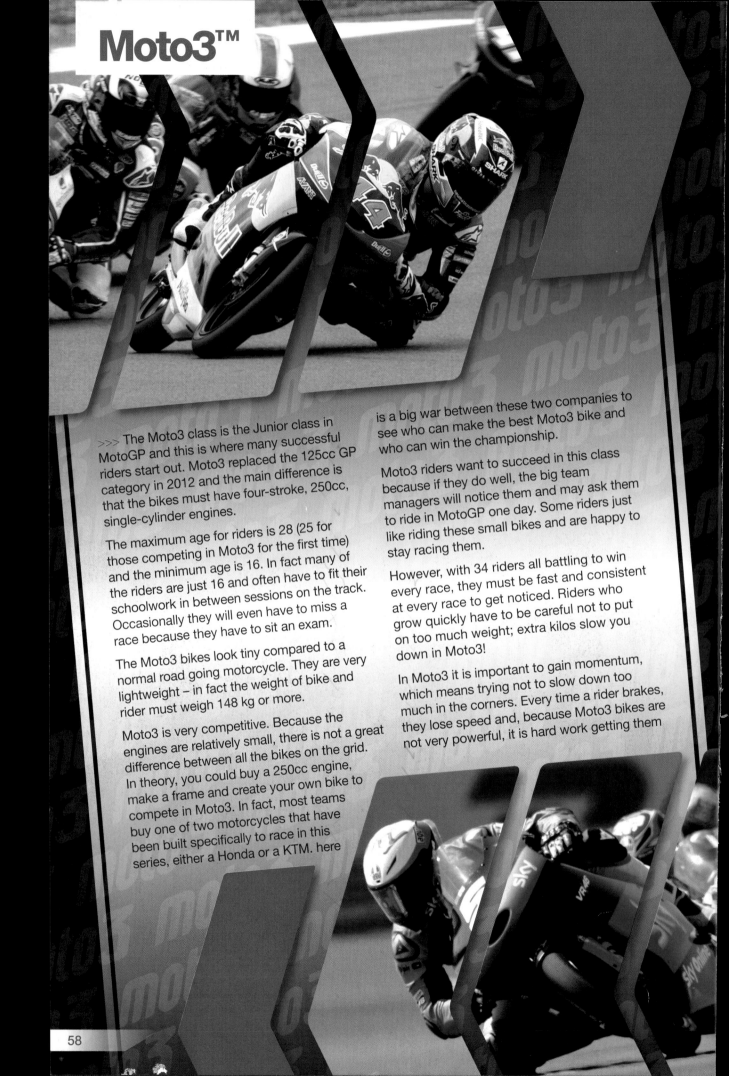

Moto3™

>>> The Moto3 class is the Junior class in MotoGP and this is where many successful riders start out. Moto3 replaced the 125cc GP category in 2012 and the main difference is that the bikes must have four-stroke, 250cc, single-cylinder engines.

The maximum age for riders is 28 (25 for those competing in Moto3 for the first time) and the minimum age is 16. In fact many of the riders are just 16 and often have to fit their schoolwork in between sessions on the track. Occasionally they will even have to miss a race because they have to sit an exam.

The Moto3 bikes look tiny compared to a normal road going motorcycle. They are very lightweight – in fact the weight of bike and rider must weigh 148 kg or more.

Moto3 is very competitive. Because the engines are relatively small, there is not a great difference between all the bikes on the grid. In theory, you could buy a 250cc engine, make a frame and create your own bike to compete in Moto3. In fact, most teams buy one of two motorcycles that have been built specifically to race in this series, either a Honda or a KTM. here

is a big war between these two companies to see who can make the best Moto3 bike and who can win the championship.

Moto3 riders want to succeed in this class because if they do well, the big team managers will notice them and may ask them to ride in MotoGP one day. Some riders just like riding these small bikes and are happy to stay racing them.

However, with 34 riders all battling to win every race, they must be fast and consistent at every race to get noticed. Riders who grow quickly have to be careful not to put on too much weight; extra kilos slow you down in Moto3!

In Moto3 it is important to gain momentum, which means trying not to slow down too much in the corners. Every time a rider brakes, they lose speed and, because Moto3 bikes are not very powerful, it is hard work getting them to go fast again. So Moto3 riders have to learn to ride through corners smoothly and as fast as possible, rather than stopping and starting.

Moto3 races are always fun to watch as the bikes are close together and you may see 5 or 6 riders on track together at the front on the last lap, all fighting for the lead. It is hard to predict which rider will win because the bikes can 'slipstream'. That means one bike can slip in directly behind another bike and gain speed while they are cushioned from the wind by the rider and bike in front. They can then pull out to one side and blast past the guy ahead of them. Because of that, you will often hear Moto3 riders saying "I don't want to be in the lead on the last lap" – and that's something you will not hear from MotoGP riders, who always want to be ahead!

Moto3™ Star: Danny Kent

>> Danny Kent is from Chippenham in England and is the most successful British Moto3 rider ever. In 2015 he won three races in a row, in America, Argentina and then in Spain.

Danny has always loved bikes and started racing when he was 6. He's competed in World Championships since 2011 and has ridden in Moto2 and Moto3. He has the potential to be MotoGP Champion in the future, so watch this space!

>>> Age: 23
>>> Weight: 68Kg
>>> Height: 176cm (5'9")
>>> Race Number #52

This is a special number for Danny. It was the race number of James Toseland, a former double World Superbike Champion and a good friend of Danny. When James was injured in a crash he found he could no longer race and Danny races with his number 52 in honour of James. James is now a rock star, so don't feel too sorry for him!

Rider Gear

Every racer chooses which equipment they wear very, very carefully. Helmets, leather race suits, gloves and boots make up a vital shell around the rider to protect them if they crash.

Their outfit will include body armour, but this is a very long way from a medieval knight's suit of armour which would be much too heavy and slow for racing.

A race kit has to be very lightweight and very flexible to allow the rider to move around on the bike as they go from corner to corner. At the same time it has to be strong and act like a barrier between the rider and anything they might hit when they fall off.

To meet all these requirements, the companies that make rider clothing spend a long, long time developing and testing materials and technology to help keep riders safe.

The Race Suit

Riders have to wear a one piece leather race suits which zips up at the front. These are made of leather, either from cow leather or, for the richer rider, kangaroo leather which is very soft and flexible. A race suit will have extra armour built into it at the knees and elbows, along the leg and lower arm. You will also see large humps on the back of each MotoGP rider's suit, to protect the back of their neck and upper back. However, you probably won't see the cleverest bit of the race suit – this is an electronic system which measures the speed the race suit is travelling at and the angle of the motorcycle it is connected to. The signals the race suit electronics constantly receive let it know if the rider has crashed. As soon as the system receives the 'crashed' signal a balloon inside the race suit inflates (within milliseconds) so that the rider has a "cushion" to protect them when they land. This technology has protected many riders when they've crashed and has saved riders from many a broken collarbone, a very common racing injury. Of course these suits are expensive; they cost thousands of pounds.

Helmet, Gloves and Boots

Riders always want the strongest crash helmet, gloves and boots, as injuries to their heads, hands and feet can be serious and prevent them from racing for a long time. At the same time, they need freedom of movement. Titanium is often used to give protection as it is very strong and light. This is combined with high quality leather, Kevlar and other special materials to each MotoGP rider's needs. Many races are held in the summer and it is important that riders stay cool during the race. Imagine riding your bike or running in a race wearing all your warmest heaviest clothes. Ventilation is built into every piece of equipment to keep our riders cool, from vents on their helmets all the way down to air holes on their boots.

Riders usually take great care of their kit and will only allow their close friends or family to handle it before a race. But if a race has gone badly for them and they have a tantrum, you may see their gloves or helmet being thrown across the garage in anger!

Answers

Wordsearch p17

```
R R M L O S A I L V G B B K
K A A D T W K P Y A G W X E
E S G V U X L K M L Q O I N
N O N J H C F H S E J L R E
O R E T M T A U H N E H P E
T D T V N N Z T R T L C D H
S E I N F U D A I I C T N S
R P M M K T P H R N Y U A Y
E I A I M S B D L O C R R R
V N R M A D R L Q R R C G R
L A E H T M K M N O O L B A
I D L P L C Z L K S T A G B
S R L F M K X R P S O C T B
F J I M T H G T D I M D G L
```

Maze: Get to the Grid p26

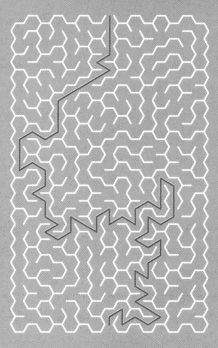

Crossword p22

```
B L A C K F L A G   H
        R       T O P S T E P           C
  M I C H E L I N   N             Q       A
        R       D         A       U       S
      A P R I L I A   P I T B O A R D     E
      R         A         A       L   T   Y
L A G U N A S E C A     M   V I S O R   R S
      C         C       A   F       I   A T
T W I S T T H E T H R O T T L E     Y   C O
    M           I       A       D A N N Y K E N T   G   N
L E A T H E R       S   S     F O U R     I   E
    R       S U S P E N S I O N         O     U
    S               A               N   R
    H                               T
  C A R B O N               W I N N I N G   O
    L                               O
                      E S P A R G A R O
                              O
                    M U G E L L O
```

What could possibly go wrong? p27

They all happened!

a. Cal Crutchlow
b. Julian Simon
c. Cal Crutchlow
d. Niklas Ajo from the Moto3 class. The rider who did this was Romano Fenati and he was punished! A very dangerous move!
e. Dani Pedrosa
f. Hiroshi Aoyama (stand in for Dani Pedrosa)
g. Jorge Lorenzo
h. Eugene Laverty
i. Maverick Vinales

Spot the Difference p52